T0209573

Discover Your
Determination

Advice for Christian Leaders
Who Love Life

COLLEEN MCLEAN

WESTBOW
PRESS®
A DIVISION OF THOMAS NELSON
& ZONDERVAN

WestBow Press books may be ordered through
booksellers or by contacting:

WestBow Press
A Division of Thomas Nelson & Zondervan
1663 Liberty Drive
Bloomington, IN 47403
www.westbowpress.com
1 (866) 928-1240

ISBN: 978-1-9736-5291-5 (sc)
ISBN: 978-1-9736-5290-8 (hc)
ISBN: 978-1-9736-5292-2 (e)

Library of Congress Control Number: 2019901224

Print information available on the last page.

WestBow Press rev. date: 2/7/2019

Contents

"Leaders Who Lead with Love"

Colleen McLean

Leaders who lead with love, like Jesus led,
Would never leave this book unread.
They are loving, lucid, and loyal,
Strong, compassionate, and joyful.
God has given them victory,
But their lives have a history
Of battles and triumphs,
Of grasshoppers and giants.
They come out winners over strife.
They are leaders who love life.

What you are about to read is the result of collecting my life's experiences in short sentences. What a privilege to be able to do so. I wish to thank and honor my lifelong mate, my wonderful husband, Peter, whom I have known since I was a child and love very much. I cannot think of anyone better to spend life with. Thank you to my family—including many grandchildren—who have provided me with heaps of material for this publication. You may recognize yourselves in here, and it is all good, so enjoy!

Introduction

This book is for everyone—for the leader, the adventurer, the lover of life, the philosopher, the coach, the teacher, the parent. You may agree with some of the sentiments and you may disagree but in it you will discover that the only person stopping you is you. You really can fulfil your dream and do life successfully because your determination makes it happen. It is especially for the thinker and the lover of God who wants answers to those hard questions. It is good to always have an answer ready when someone asks you about the hope you have.[1]

I was a Scripture teacher in State Schools on the Central Coast of NSW, Australia, for more than ten years, and I found that there was always one or two students who had a question for me, either inside the classroom or outside on the playground.

A favorite question was, "Miss, what is the meaning of life?"

Knowing I was being set up, I would have my answer ready, and in my best teacher voice, I would say, "Thank you for asking me this very good question. I am about to tell you the easy answer. Are you ready for this?"

Anticipation would build, and I would glance at their eager faces and begin my reply. "Many people would say that the meaning of life is to be happy. But the real meaning for your life is Jesus Christ inside you because your life has its meaning in the One who created it."

It was not the answer they were expecting, but it was an answer that contains a great truth:

"For in him we live and move and have our being" (Acts 17:28).

We all come from God, and when we believe in Him, we live in God. And when we die, we go back to God. This is the simple meaning of life. However, your life in God will be a roller coaster: there will ups and downs; it will be exciting, radical, worth every minute; and God promises to never leave you through the whole lot. You will do things you never thought possible, because you can trust Him to never let you down. The Bible is full of amazing stories of ordinary people who trusted God, and even though they failed once or twice, they achieved remarkable things. You can find them for yourself in the pages of the most read book in the world—the Bible. To start, try Abraham; Deborah; King David; Mary, the mother of Jesus; or the apostles Peter and Paul.

I have found that religion has complicated some very simple truths and made Christianity boring and hard to understand. It is not hard to understand that Our Father God is really, really good. He is a million, trillion times better than you think He is, and He just wants to love you. It is not hard to understand that His love will make you a million times better. It is not hard to understand that there is no strategy of the devil; there is nothing in existence right now in heaven or on earth that can separate you from God's love.[2] It is not hard to understand that Jesus bought your sin—not to bring it up again but to destroy it so you don't have to think about it anymore.[3] It is not hard to understand that you are going to heaven, and hell is not your destination because you are completely and forever forgiven. It is not hard to understand that if we think of ourselves as sinners and always recall the bad things we did, we will stop ourselves from stepping into the normal Christian life God has planned for us.

We don't understand sometimes because cares and concerns can blind our eyes and rob us of the time we need to really sit down and fully understand the wonderful truths of the Gospel. We don't understand sometimes because we find contradictions and hypocrisy. So let this publication make life easier for you, but please don't take my word for it; check the answers out for yourself.

Enjoy!
Much love,
Colleen

Chapter 1

For the Leader in You

To get started, I will share my five fabulous, fruitful, fundamental, functional, faultless, fearless, and favorite foundations for leaders who love life.

1. Admit when you've made a mistake. The first life lesson for leaders who love life is to be able to admit you make mistakes, because people expect leaders to do the right thing. Leaders who love life will,

from time to time, make mistakes. That's life! So the best words you can learn are "Oops!" and "Sorry!" And don't forget this: "Forgive me. I got that wrong. Please allow me to apologize." And this: "Sorry. My mistake. How can I fix this?" When you admit your mistake, most people will say, "Oh, that's okay. I've done that too. No worries!"

2. Lead with love. Make it safe for others to use their talents. Protect them by taking the hits yourself, and then confront them privately in a caring manner. When faced with a conflict, act quickly and never let it simmer too long. Support, encourage, and let others know that you are on their team. Listen, learn from them, reward them, and above all, lead. Be the responsible leader of the pack. The result will be that you look good and your organization succeeds because everyone is doing his or her job well.

3. Forgive. Forgiving others for their mistakes is doing the right thing. When you forgive, move on, build a bridge (even with one plank at a time), and get over it. Remember, you may want to cross that bridge one day, so try not to burn it. However, keep in mind there are certain bridges that should be burned.

4. Ask for advice. If you find yourself in a leadership position, still ask for advice. Take counsel with humility.

5. Live by the Golden Rule. These wonderful words were spoken by Jesus in Matthew 7:12: "Whatever you want men to do to you, do also to them."

Chapter 2

One-Liners for Leaders

Only you can determine your attitude.

Leadership is more than a title.

The best way to lose the ability to influence people is to boss them around.

People can choose whether to follow your leadership.

You can tame lions, and even dogs can round up sheep, but if you try to do the same with people, it will turn into disaster.

People will trust you if you believe in them, but they will feel controlled if you try to fix them.

Try understanding and assertiveness instead of force, fear, manipulation, and control.

Lead *with* love, not *for* love.

Deal with one problem at a time, and things get resolved.

Build people and not empires, and then people will build your empire.

Criticizing someone will not motivate him or her to change. It hurts and angers the other person.

When you lead by example and encouragement, people will want to do what is right.

Your role as a leader is never to set out to fix people but to serve them.

Never tolerate evil.

People think that if they sack the coach, the leader, or the prime minister, everything will be okay. But maybe not. Think about it.

People like to express their views about their leader's flaws but rarely express their views of his or her strengths.

By the way, everyone deserves criticism, but it is all too often negative.

Learn to listen. It is worth it.

Take the time and make the effort to understand others' points of view. They will know you value them if you listen.

There are two good reasons to listen:

1. You learn something.

2. People respond to those who listen to them.

Everyone wants to have his or her point of view heard; your point of view is not the only one.

It is hard to make friends with people who do not listen.

Serving is the goal, and respect is the way to serve.

When dealing with people, stick to the facts.

All you can know about anybody is what you see or what that person tells you.

You have the right to judge only if you are smarter than God. When Jesus said in Luke 6:37, "Judge not, and you shall not be judged." He meant it!

It is better to ask questions than it is to judge.

God alone knows why people do what they do.

Problems happen to everyone, so don't waste your time trying to figure out why. You will be wrong.

If you cannot confront in love, you are not ready to confront.

The first law of confrontation is this: get rid of all the judgments you have heard or made concerning the person. Deal with facts.

The goal of confrontation must be to help that person as much as to help yourself. You win. The other person wins. Everyone comes out a winner!

When you want to convince someone who does not want to be convinced, back off and have a good day instead.

If you feel a person can be convinced, begin with what you agree on.

Here's something I have learned about myself: I can't fix anyone. People fix themselves! I have enough trouble fixing myself. If I take care of myself first, then I can help others. *Maybe.*

Here's something I have learned: trying to change people causes too much stress. Stop trying and save your own life!

Trying to control circumstances causes too much stress. Stop it, and save everyone's lives!

Everything does not have to go your way, and happiness does not come by making people do what you want.

It is best to stick to facts and not exaggerate.

Sometimes it is wise to keep your opinion to yourself.

Your behavior affects everyone, including yourself.

Practice being humble, and when it comes to playing second fiddle, you won't stumble.

Humility does not happen by accident.

Be humble on purpose—do not exalt yourself higher than you ought.

Demeaning yourself is not humility; it is demeaning.

It is not prideful to recognize and acknowledge your awesome talents.

Take pride in who you are and what you achieve.

Offense is no reason to be offensive.

You don't have to live up to what people think of you.

Never pass on a rumor.

Always tell the truth.

When someone says something negative about you, just deny it. Tell the truth of the matter. Be honest!

Negative talk creates a space that can be taken by more negative words.

Attitude is the difference between a good day and a not-so-good day. It is up to you.

Gentleness? Do it lots!

Violence? Knock it off! The only thing to do with anger is stop—*now,* before it gets ugly.

We get back more than we give. Be careful what you give.

Two wrongs never make a right.

Keep your promises, and then you won't let people down.

Ignore the negative looks you get; that way you look better than the looks you get!

Double standards equal double trouble.

People do stuff because of who they are, not because of you.

You don't have to be afraid to say no for fear that people won't love you. You can just say, "How about no?"

You can say no and still feel good about yourself.

You can say, "No, thanks," as many times as you like.

When you say no, stick to it!

You can say, "Yes, thanks," especially when you are offered something yummy!

When you say yes, stick to it!

Indecisiveness can leave you open to being taken advantage of, and it can happen quickly.

Accept the consequences of your decision. Hopefully, you will consider these before you make a decision.

You can do whatever you like, but not everything is good for you.

Little things build up, so you have to address them as they happen.

It is better to tell people the truth, even if it hurts their feelings.

Telling the truth does not make you a dragon!

You can't go forward by looking back. To go ahead, you need to look ahead!

It is all too easy to be preoccupied with your own troubles. Stop it now. Life is not always easy!

Focus is the ability to ignore distractions and pursue only what is important.

More people are *for* you than *against* you.

How you treat people has a lot to do with who you think you are.

If you are concerned about what others think of you when you are competing, you get choked up and limit your chances of giving your best.

If you dwell on mistakes, even those from a minute ago, you lose concentration and limit your chances of giving your best.

If you set a goal within your limits, you win even if you lose because you know that you did your best and reached your goal.

You hear what you want to hear, and you see what you want to see.

You look for and find the evidence of what you already believe.

You can see and not see.

You can hear and not hear.

To think you can get away with something wrong because there is a good reason it is wrong.

You cannot lead others if you can't lead yourself.

Talking is better than texting because not everyone can spell "laughing out loud" properly.

The real you is not Photoshopped.

Freedom of speech is feared by people who know they are wrong.

New Year's resolutions are really new rules to change your behavior for the new year.

Your words can get you (and others) into more trouble than your actions can.

Always recognize and reward volunteers.

Nobody is equally gifted at everything, and everyone's time is limited.

Not many people just volunteer. Many are invited or coerced to volunteer through personal contact, so be nice to them.

It is better not to have a lot of bosses; let the volunteer be responsible and take ownership of his or her job. Too many cooks do spoil the broth.

It is better to not let someone volunteer for too many jobs. When someone does too much, someone else does less.

Volunteers can make mistakes, but it is good to remember that there are two basic things about mistakes:

1. We all make them;

2. We are quite happy to be the one to point them out to others.

Mistakes occur when under pressure. The answer? Get over it and get on with living.

Admit your mistakes before someone else points them out to you.

Rejoicing over the mistakes of others is a mistake.

Chapter 3

For the Adventurer in You

Only you can determine your attitude.

Have a go at something or you may never know if you can.

Just have a go; life is meant to be lived to the extreme!

Life is to be enjoyed, not endured.

God gave us brains and muscles and emotions and enthusiasm and holiness to actually use.

Life is what you have been given; existing and extreme living is a choice. Go for it!

Loosen up and enjoy living!

You have the right to do what you want, but you have to live with the consequences.

If you think you are beaten, you are.

If you limit what you can do, you limit what you do.

When you make excuses, you set limits on yourself.

Stop making excuses, and face the facts.

I don't have what it takes, but the God inside me does.

You cannot have a chance without taking a risk.

You cannot achieve the victory until the end of the game.

If you sit and wait for something to happen, nothing will happen.

If you do not venture, you remain ordinary.

If you have never tried and failed, you have never taken a risk.

Fear can immobilize you, and the longer you stay fearful, the harder it is to get over.

The fear of making a mistake is worse than any mistake you will ever make.

Treat the embarrassment of a mistake the same as you treat an annoying fly—flick it away. Everybody makes mistakes.

Fear really is all about you, so you really do need to get over yourself.

Fear can be disguised as hesitancy, or being wise, or waiting on God for an answer.

Be adventurous with your giving.

Give cheerfully, not begrudgingly, and then your generosity counts.

When you give to others, you enrich yourself.

You can work your own miracles with money by giving it away.

Something happens inside you when you give, and something happens inside the ones you give it to. Miraculous! Try it!

Chapter 4

For the Parent in You

Only you can determine your attitude.

Love your children no matter what!

Motherhood is the hardest job in the entire world.

Never ask a mom where or if she works.

A tidy house has no children living in it.

You cannot get your point across by being cross.

You cannot please everyone by trying to please everyone.

You cannot make peace by keeping peace.

There are two main issues in life: money and relationships.

The money issue is simple: be generous with it.

Relationships are simple: they cost lots of time, not necessarily money.

Children should obey their parents!

Young ones should never say their parents are stupid, because that is a stupid thing to say.

Older ones should never say, "In my day, we did it this way," because it is still their day.

Middle-aged ones should never say never—because you never know.

Look after your loving parents in their old age because they lovingly looked after you in your youth.

Cleaning is cleaning until it is clean.

The bedroom is not tidy until it is tidy.

Chapter 5

For the Philosopher in You

Only you can determine your attitude.

Sometimes you need to take a break and have a fresh look at your life.

Sometimes you have to endure stuff, so try to find a way to enjoy it.

You can forgive people, or you can hold it against them, or you can ignore them.

It is easier to forgive and move on.

Forgiving does not make what they did okay, it makes you feel better.

You have to forgive if you want peace in your heart.

Unforgiveness, bitterness, resentment, rejection, and envy can make you sick.

Unforgiveness keeps you from moving on.

It is a privilege to forgive.

Forgive, and be free to move on with your life!

Freedom is the power to choose.

Bitter people usually don't have a lot of friends.

Bitterness touches those we love the most.

Real heroes are acknowledged after they die.

Try *hard* love because it is better than no love at all.

If you talk a lot, you'll probably say something you'll regret.

Memorizing stuff is not enough. You have to act on that knowledge if you want results.

Should "shouldn't" be in the dictionary! Because you shouldn't tell people what they should do because you don't live in their shoes. You don't have the whole story, so you should help them find out what they should do for themselves.

Change for the better is difficult. That is why 95 percent of people never change. But change for the better can bring excitement and growth, so do it!

If you are not prepared to follow the rules, then clearly, rules are not that important to you, unless you are disadvantaged by them. So admit it and decide to follow rules—it is the best thing for everyone, including you.

Think about this: giving control of your life to another person or organization means you have to obey them. Rather, use self-control and choose to keep the rules because you want to, not because you have to.

If you want to change and experience growth on the inside, put yourself in situations outside of your comfort zone. You'll love it!

You don't have to agree, but when you are adamant that you are right, your attitude will be condescending and ugly. Did you get that? UGLEEE!

Did you realize the chances of different people agreeing with each other 100 percent of the time is very slim. You have permission to disagree.

"Yes" says I agree, and "but" says I disagree. What you are really saying is that it is not your fault. It *is* your fault, actually! You are saying,

"Yes, but," to give you time to make up an excuse for it not being your fault.

It is okay for boys and men to cry. Jesus wept openly!

Chapter 6

For the Coach in You

Only you can determine your attitude toward coaching.

You cannot coach anyone if they don't want to be coached.

Passion comes by believing with your heart, not just your mind.

Passion without knowledge will produce a team of energetic people going in circles and not achieving anything.

If you're not enthusiastic about something, no one else will be either.

If you are lukewarm, you and your team will never boil.

Want to be enthusiastic? Then hang around someone who is.

Encouragement is the action of giving someone support, confidence, and hope.

Favoritism on the part of the coach breeds division.

Everyone is important.

The key to discipline lies in consistency.

The key to consistency is to have a plan.

The key to staying calm and maintaining that consistency is to have a plan.

Look ahead!

Penalties can be turned into opportunities.

Setbacks can become comebacks.

Rules rule on the sporting field.

Consequences cost.

Bad behavior is boring.

Good sportsmanship wins more awards than winning the championship.

Question: What is the difference between an obstacle and an opportunity?

Answer: Your attitude toward it! The way you look at it! Every opportunity has a difficulty, and every difficulty has an opportunity.

Question: Which is true: *"change brings growth"* or *"growth brings change"*?

Answer: Change brings growth, if your attitude is right. A positive attitude will bring change, but a negative attitude will also bring change.

The Positive Coach

- Set goals;
- Plans and carries them out;
- Backs up the plan with vision and positive words;
- Writes it down;
- Develops vision;
- Lives it passionately;
- Embraces change and believes it can be done;
- Is motivated by a belief in achieving;
- Expects the best;
- Looks for accomplishment;
- Gives encouragement;
- Gives recognition promptly and sincerely;
- Describes the positives and the errors;
- Tells how positives affect the team; and
- Expresses appreciation.

The Negative Coach

- Sets goals
- Plans and carries them out
- Backs up the plan with vision

- Writes it down
- Does not back up with positive words
- Offers no development of vision
- Forgets about it
- Fears change;
- Says maybe;
- Is motivated by fear of losing;
- Accepts whatever comes;
- Looks at the problem;
- Complains and blames;
- Rarely gives recognition;
- Describes the errors;
- Doesn't recognize the positive effect; and
- Expects to be thanked.

Chapter 7

God Stuff

Only you can determine your attitude toward God.

Your circumstances do not dictate who you are.

Your looks do not determine who you are.

Your past does not determine who you are.

Your address does not determine who you are.

Your financial state does not determine who you are.

Your ethnicity does not determine who you are.

Your life story or the long tale of your triumphs do not determine who you are.

You are who God says you are.

You are a son or daughter of the Most High God, with equal rights, because He lives in you.[4]

Think about yourself often, but make sure it lines up with what God says about you because you can't afford to think differently.

The heart is where you believe and doubt.

You harden your heart by closing your mind.

Build monuments in your heart to God.

The problem with some of us is that we don't reveal the God life inside us, we just reveal our personality.

Jesus knows how to fix you; He knows how to still the storm; He has done it before.[5]

Confession is basically agreeing with God that He is always right.

Identifying sin in someone is not judging; it is better to confront than let another continue in sin.

Truth is nothing to be afraid of—true!

Even though God is exalted in power and majesty, He wants to be friends with you.

Father God is good; He is like Jesus: He heals you and does not make you sick to make you better.

Christians are the Church, so whatever Christians do is what the Church is doing.

Faith requires a risk.

Faith can make you a hero.

If you can get your faith working and be obedient to the truth, you can succeed in whatever God places before you.

You don't have to believe for you to have something, you have to believe you have it.

God's promises to you keep you on the right track, so what you do with His promises matter.

Jesus carried a cross so you don't have to.

It is more blessed to give than receive[6] because if you give from a pure heart, God will bless you and your gift.

God owns everything; it all belongs to Him. You are just looking after it!

Holiness is not an option, because God makes you holy.[7]

Perfection was never God's plan for your life— holiness is!

The first person Jesus revealed Himself to as the Messiah was a woman from Samaria, and she was the first-ever evangelist.[8]

When we forget what God has done for us, we forget Him.

We forget because we didn't give Him significance.

Focus on something bigger than you—God—and then you won't think about yourself too much! In the beginning, God; in the middle, God; in the end, God. God is number one, number two, and number three.

There is absolutely nothing you can do to make God love you more or love you less.

God's love demonstrates how valuable you are, not your works.

God is okay with you feeling His love.

You can know about God from the Bible, but you know Him personally through experiencing Him personally.

Keeping the rules alone will never make you right, but having Jesus in your heart will.

Working harder, keeping rules, and doing penance to feel better about yourself is hard. Work hard at building a relationship with God instead.

Live in a romance with God, and then you will love yourself properly.

God's eyes are on you.

Keep your eyes on Him.

When God gives you a gift, take it and unwrap it and use it.

God will ignore your fear and expect you to do what He has set out for you to do.

God is not impressed by reputations.

I belong to a kingdom where a man is not more privileged than a woman.[9] Do you?

Since you were created by God, you were also made for His kingdom and its lifestyle; therefore, it is possible to live right.

You are worth the price Jesus paid for you, which means you are worthy to receive everything God has for you.

God is not your enemy. He is not angry with anyone.

Jesus was born in an animal stall, and God was not surprised or horrified.

Getting your facts right about God does not make you right with God.

Hell was prepared for the devil and his demons.

It is not hard to understand that Our Father God is really, really good. He is a million trillion times better than you think He is, and He just wants to love you.

It is not hard to understand that His love will make all of you a million times better.

It is not hard to understand that there is no strategy of the devil, that there is nothing in existence right now in heaven or on earth that can separate you from the love of God.[10]

It is not hard to understand that Jesus bought your sin—not to bring it up again but to destroy it so you don't have to think about it anymore.[11]

It is not hard to understand that you are going to heaven, and hell is not your destination because you are completely and forever forgiven.

It is not hard to understand that if we think of ourselves as sinners and always recall the bad things we did, we will stop ourselves from stepping into the normal Christian life God has planned for us.

God is so real! He created your unique DNA, and that makes you important because all life has its foundation in the One who created it.[12]

Who made God? Nobody! God has always existed. God was always there and always will be.

There is a built-in need for us to worship something bigger than ourselves.

You cannot get to heaven without Jesus.[13]

You don't become an angel in heaven when you die.

Angels are God's servants; they do many things that help people, but only on God's command. An angel rolled away the stone from Jesus's tomb, but it was Jesus who destroyed the power of death by God raising Him to life.

Jesus changes lives. Billions of people around the world can testify to it.

Jesus was friends with prostitutes, adulterers, thieves, liars, and drunks, and the religious people hated Him.

Our freedom of choice is valuable to God.

God hears every prayer you have prayed and has heard the prayers of every person in the whole world.

Every person is valued equally by God. The Bible tells us that all people are equal.[14]

Chapter 8

Answers to Questions I've Been Asked

Q: What is the meaning of life?

A: All humans know they are going to die one day, and that they somehow have to make themselves happy along the way. Many people would say this is the meaning of life. The real meaning of life, however, has its foundation in the One who created it. God is the author of your life, so having God in your life gives it meaning.[15]

Q: What's the plan and purpose of my existence?

A: God's plan for you is massive. I'm not kidding. This will blow your socks off! His plan for you is that you grow up into the likeness of Jesus himself.[16] So God's plan for your life is wild, huge, and even unbelievable, but it is true. Told ya! God knew you before you were born. He knows your heart better than you do. You were fearfully and wonderfully made by Him, and His eye has been on you all the time. You are precious in His eyes.[17] And a whole lot more.

Q: How did God create the universe?

A: God created the universe by His word![18]

Q: Does God still sustain the universe?

A: God sustains the universe by His Word! He is Lord of Heaven and earth,[19] and He gives life and breath to all things. He spoke it into existence and has never unspoken it.[20]

Q: How do you know the Bible is true?

A: There are about seven to thirteen manuscripts of Plato and about 120 manuscripts of Aristotle. When Plato and Aristotle are quoted, we accept their sayings as accurate. The New Testament is better established than any book. It is unique! It has been preserved in more manuscripts than any other ancient work of literature, with more than 5,800 complete or fragmented Greek manuscripts catalogued. There are more than two hundred biblical manuscripts among the Dead Sea Scrolls.[21] The Jews in the Old Testament, consisting of the nation of Israel, received the Old Testament books as coming from God, and we received it from them.

Q: How is the Gospel different to other philosophical writings?

A: The Gospel is different from any other philosophy in the world because it focuses on a single person, Jesus Christ. The Bible is different from any other of the religious writings in the world because the whole Bible from start to finish focuses on a single person, Jesus Christ. The Bible is *the* bestseller in the world because it is the only book translated into every language.

Q: Why do people hurt each other?

A: People hurt each other because it is a part of life and no one misses out. We have all been hurt sometime or other, and the key is not to give that hurt importance. It is what you do with the hurt that matters.

Q: Why do people have so much hate?

A: Hate is always a choice we are free to make.

Q: Why do bad things happen to good people?

A: Things happen for many reasons, including our poor choices and bad decisions. Scripture says in Galatians 6:7 "Do not be deceived, God is not mocked; for whatever a man sows, that he will also reap." So whatever we give out, we will get back. However, there is a promise that God works all things together for good.[22] All things means all your problems, cares, trials, and worries. Bad things do happen to good people. In fact, bad things happen to everyone. They just happen! God makes the sun to rise on the evil and on the good and sends rain on the just and on the unjust.[23] It is what you do with those things that determine how you come out the other end. The Bible says in 1 Peter 5:7 "cast all your care upon Him, for He cares for you." God didn't say He would remove every problem or spare us from our stupid selves or any disaster but that He would be watching over us through it all, and delighting in us when we overcome. *Yay!*[24] And He can bring good out of bad.[25]

Q: Does God make you sick?

A: God cannot make people sick because He does not have sickness to give away. People just get sick; it is a fact of life. God does not make you sick so He can make you better. God does not make you sick to teach you a lesson. That's silly! Jesus healed sick people all the time.[26]

Q: Does God kill people because He wants them in heaven?

A: Jesus raised people from the dead, so it is not God's will for anyone to die before his or her time. Tragedies, disease, disasters, and accidents just happen, and they are not from God. Jesus told us that God is light and doesn't have any darkness in him.[27]

Q: Does God punish people?

A: God does not punish anyone. God lovingly tries to correct, just as any father would.[28] However, people do a good job at criticizing and punishing.

Q: Why are there terrible diseases in the world?

A: We live in a world that is imperfect! When God created the world, it was perfect and perfectly good, and then the man and woman he created to be perfect sinned and messed up God's perfect plan, and sickness and disease was allowed in. But the good news is that Jesus heals sick people.[29] [30]

Q: Why is it so difficult to understand God?

A: It is not difficult to understand God. But well-intentioned people have complicated some very simple truths over the centuries. Jesus did some spectacular miracles but there were religious people who could not understand because they willfully closed their hearts against the truth,[31] and that is why some might find it difficult to understand even today.

You get to heaven by believing and accepting what Jesus did for you! Easy![32] Just being good and obeying the commandments won't get you to heaven, because there is no way anyone can obey every commandment for a lifetime. There is no way any of us can make ourselves right before God, so we need a Savior who has already done that for us—Jesus.[33]

Q: Why is sin so bad?

A: Sin is bad because it is not good for you and it hurts others, it makes you feel guilty, and it gives the devil a reason to annoy you.[34] It makes your life messy. Anything that is used by people for the purpose to which God did not intend for it to be used is wrong—adultery, lying, stealing, cheating, sodomy, and gossiping are all equally wrong. But there is unlimited forgiveness and peace from God when we confess our sins to Him.

Q: What is hell all about?

A: Hell is the other place the Bible talks about,[35] and it is also eternal. Jesus said that hell was prepared for the devil and his angels. God's desire is that people should not end up in hell because hell was not originally intended for people.[36] Hell is a place of torment, a pit of darkness,[37] because God is not there.

Q: How does God communicate with us?

A: God communicates with us in our language. God created Adam and Eve with a language. He can be heard as just a thought in your mind.[38]

Q: Does God know everything?

A: God knows everything. He knew you before you were born, and He knows the secrets of your heart.[39] He even knows what we are thinking,[40] and God already knows what you need before you ask him.[41] God is all-knowing.[42]

Q: What is repentance?

A: Repentance is a decision that you make; it is changing your mind about the way you behave.

Q: What is the kingdom of God?

A: Jesus said His kingdom was not of this world. It has no buildings or walls; it is inside you if Jesus lives in you.

Q: What about sex outside of marriage?

A: God's ways are best and the safest, and it is to your advantage to do things His way. God means for sex to be a gift for marriage because it is an intimate part of a relationship between a husband and wife where the two become one, emotionally and spiritually. In marriage, it is a bond they share that strengthens friendship and love.

Q: Is Satan responsible for the evil in the world?

A: No! Satan is not responsible for all the evil in the world. God gave humans the power and freedom to create evil. We all have free choice to create good or to create evil, and choices have consequences, good and bad. That is life!

Q: Did the people who killed Jesus make a real choice, or were they not responsible because it was God's plan?

A: No, the Bible insists that they were completely responsible for doing what they did. Yet it was also God's plan.[43] God knew how to arrange evil men and their choices to serve his own good purpose. Of course, God also knew how to raise his Son from the dead.

Q: Is it easy being a Christian?

A: Yes and no! No because God's Spirit doesn't make cowards out of us. Yes because the Spirit gives us power, love, and self-control.[44] And no because God did not choose us to be sinful but to be pure and holy,[45] and that's not easy but definitely possible.

Q: Is Jesus relevant today?

A: Jesus is relevant today because during His life, Jesus experienced all the troubles that you face and so understands how you feel.[46] Jesus is alive today and vitally interested in your life as much as He was with His disciples when He walked around with them.

Q: Is Jesus all sweetness and light?

A: Another lie we might have believed is that Jesus is all sweetness and light. It is true there is no darkness is Him;[47] however, He is the Lion of the tribe of Judah, and when He walked the earth as a man He was a countercultural radical who raised the dead, healed the sick, and liberated the oppressed. He angered the religious leaders so much they schemed to kill Him. He went against the culture of His day by talking to women, touching dead people and lepers, and allowing a woman with an issue of blood to touch Him, all of which were outlawed. He made friends with prostitutes, corrupt tax collectors, blind beggars, and cripples. He even washed filthy feet. He made wine for drunk people and called the religious leaders hypocrites and "whitewashed tombs".[48] He never excluded anyone, and He healed everyone who came to Him.

Q: Does the devil make me do bad stuff?

A: Here is another lie that we might have believed—that the devil creates the evil and makes me do it. We always have a choice. If we listen to and believe lies, we are actually choosing to process them into reality inside our brains, and in doing so, we create the evil and act upon it. But we don't have to believe the lie, so that makes us accountable for the decisions we make and the lies we believe.[49]

Q: Is there anything God cannot do?

A: There are some things that God cannot do. He cannot lie, sin, or deny Himself.[50] However, God is all powerful and can bring to pass the impossible.[51]

Q: If the Commandment says "You shall not kill," how do you explain how the Old Testament people of God killed everyone in an enemy city?

A: This is such a good question and I know this answer is not sufficient for "the thinker in you." I don't know what the answer is, but there are explanations. Firstly, God loved Israel and would keep the oath He swore to Abraham. He did not want His chosen people to be like the other nations or be influenced by them. He wanted a people who were separated to Himself. He chose them because He loved them and wanted them to obey Him in all things, so that the Savior Jesus would come through them for our sakes.[52] Secondly, does the Bible say, "You shall not kill" or "You shall not murder"?

Exodus 20:13 says, "You shall not murder." So the next question should be …

Q: Is there a difference between killing and murder?

A: Murder is where there is malice and forethought. It is the unlawful premeditated killing of a human by another. Merriam-Webster Dictionary defines murder as "the crime of unlawfully killing a person especially with malice aforethought." God told the Israelites to go to war. Read about it here:

> So the people shouted when the priests blew the trumpets. And it happened when the people heard the sound of the trumpet, and the people shouted with a great shout, that the wall fell down flat. Then the people went up into the city, every man straight before him, and they took the city. And they utterly destroyed all that was in the city, both man

and woman, young and old, ox and
sheep and donkey, with the edge of
the sword." (Joshua 6:21–22)

All the people, except for Rahab, all the
livestock, everything was destroyed at Jericho,
but the silver, gold, bronze, and iron were to be
put in the treasury of the Lord. No one could
take anything for himself.[53] In Japan in World
War 2, America dropped a bomb that utterly
destroyed every dwelling and took the lives of
146,000 people.[54] Israel only did this three times,
in Jericho, Ai, and Hazor. Ai was the second
Canaanite city to be completely destroyed.
Hazor was a stronghold of the Canaanites; the
city of Hazor was taken and occupied by the
Israelites. The extermination of these tribes,
however, was never fully carried out. Jerusalem
was not taken until the time of David.[55]

Q: Why would God order the complete
destruction of the Canaanites?

A: Scripture tells us that God spared the
Amorites for four hundred years; He let the

iniquity of the Amorites keep rising up. "The iniquity of the Amorites is not yet complete" (Genesis 15:16). God sent Israel to destroy them, so Israel became an instrument of God to destroy their culture because it was wicked.

Q: Are war and killing justified?

A: Most people would agree that when Hitler was killing millions of Jews, he needed to be stopped, and therefore, this would be a good cause to go to war. Ecclesiastes chapter 3 says there's a time and a season for everything: There is a time for peace and a time for war. There's a time for love and a time for hate. The New Testament tells us to hate evil, not evil people, and to do good to those who hate us.[56]

Q: Is the account of creation in Genesis believable?

A: The New Testament refers to Genesis more than two hundred times, and it is the only book that provides an account of how life and the universe began. So we can believe it or not, and maybe we should ask the question, is evolution believable? Science has not shown the evolution of any new species or any new genetic information that would be necessary for primates to evolve into humans. Fossils indicate that there have been apes, and there have been men, but there have never been ape-men. Scientists have been proven wrong. In the 1870s, brontosaurus was exposed as a fraud. Nebraska Man was supposed to be the missing link but turned out to be a fraud.[57] Then scientists discovered Piltdown man, but he was later proved to be one of the most successful and consequential hoaxes in scientific history.[58] You can believe that "In the beginning God created the heavens and the earth" (Genesis 1:1), and you can believe that on the sixth day God said, "Let the earth bring forth the living creature according to its kind: cattle and creeping thing and beast of the earth, each according to its kind," and it was so (Genesis 1:24). Then God said, "Let us make man in Our image, according to Our likeness; let them have dominion over the fish of the sea, over the birds of the air, and over the cattle, over all the earth and over every creeping thing that creeps on the earth" (Genesis 1:26). Or you can believe, "In the beginning, who really knows for sure?"

Q: What does the Bible say regarding euthanasia/ assisted suicide/mercy killing?

A: I cannot find any scripture that speaks of compassionate murder, even at the person's request. Scripture clearly reveals that intentional murder of an innocent human being is not acceptable.[59]

Q: What about an eye for an eye and a tooth for a tooth?

A: This is saying that the punishment is equal to the crime. Remember, in the days of Leviticus where this comes from, they did not have prisons, or at least very few (Joseph did time in prison, but only the king had prisons). Jesus said in Matthew 5:38, "You have heard that it was said, 'An eye for an eye and a tooth for a tooth.' But I tell you not to resist an evil person. But whoever slaps you on your right cheek, turn the other to him also. If anyone wants to sue you and take away your tunic, let him have your cloak also. And whoever compels you to go one mile, go with him two." Jesus went beyond the law and called his followers to a higher standard of living, which is by His grace.

Q: How do you explain the Old Testament where the patriarchs had many wives?

A: God does not approve of polygamy. But people in ancient times did have polygamous relationships. Abraham with Sarah and Hagar, Jacob with Rachael and Leah, Bilhah the handmaid, David, etc. God's design for marriage is one man and one woman, where two become one.[60] Solomon had seven hundred wives and three hundred concubines, and he was the wisest man ever, but he eventually turned his back on God and indulged in the very things that he warned the young men against (e.g., adultery and worshipping other

gods were the very things he participated in).
Polygamy was acknowledged in the Mosaic
law but discouraged. This law protected the
unloved wife, and her children received part
of the inheritance.[61]

Q: Does God use women in leadership?

A: Yes! God appointed Deborah as leader,
judge, and prophetess of Israel.[62] Deborah was
a prophetess, she was married and she was the
appointed leader of the nation of Israel. People
came to her to get court cases decided. She told
men what to do and was approved by God. In the
New Testament, Priscilla was a pastor/teacher
along with her husband, Aquila.[63] Phoebe was
a leader in the church at Cenchreae.[64] Junia was
an apostle.[65] Lydia ran a house church.[66]

Q: I don't see this happening in some churches
today. Why?

A: Many churches have embraced women
in leadership, but history has shown this
has not always been the case. It is a hard

question to answer in a sentence because it goes against centuries of the status quo. All I can say here is that God most definitely did not invent a two-tier value system for men and women, men did! In the time between the testaments, scribes and Pharisees invented a religion called Judaism, which was much more restrictive and completely different compared to the Old Testament writings. Judaism had 613 commandments, many of which placed men in unreal positions of superiority, making women and girls inferior. This was the environment Jesus was born into. In first-century Israel, women were the most oppressed people; they were second-class citizens on the same level as slaves. They were not educated, had no vote or political influence, and could not even be a witness in court. However, Jesus came to set the oppressed free.[67] He ministered to women, taught them, and included them among His followers.[68] He allowed a menstruating woman to touch Him, allowed a woman to wash his feet with her tears, and allowed another to anoint Him with expensive, fragrant oil. He accepted a drink from a Samaritan woman and cast seven demons out of prostitute who followed Him to the cross and the grave. He went against the culture of His day and changed lives completely. He touched lepers and dead people, which was unacceptable. He was a countercultural radical man! So my point is, if what we do today does not line up with the life and teaching of Jesus Christ, then it is a lie.

Q: What about those verses from Paul's letters that restrict women?

A: Paul restricted women in Corinth, Ephesus, and Crete, but he wrote six other letters that encouraged women to learn, prophesy, and participate alongside men. As far as I can see, the other thirty-nine authors who contributed to the Bible did not restrict women from leadership or the top jobs at all. Good Bible study forces us to look at what was happening in Corinth, Ephesus, and Crete to find our answers. We have to look at the culture of the day, the context, who Paul was writing to, and why. And remember to apply all scripture in a way that is empowering, not down-putting. God does not look at gender when He is handing out gifts and does not restrict half of His Church from leadership roles, because we are all one in Him.[69]

Q: Does God only use women in leadership because there are no good men?

A: Absolutely not! It is demeaning and not true to say at any time that God only uses a woman because there isn't a good man. Women were leaders in the first-century church, and good men abounded.

Q: Do Christian wives really have to submit to husbands?

A: In my capacity as a marriage celebrant, I have been part of a conversation with a group of professional celebrants. One celebrant made a comment that horrified everyone, which went like this: "I was conducting a wedding, and a pastor interrupted the proceedings, pointed at the bride, and said, 'You have to submit to him!'"

The celebrant commented that it was embarrassing for the bride and the guests. Everyone looked at me for an explanation. What do I say? I thought, *Do I ignore this and brush it off, or what?* I fumbled for an answer and came up with: "How rude of the pastor. This was an unacceptable intrusion, and apart from the idea that he has taken this from the Bible, it was taken right out of context, as the verse immediately before says to submit to each other."

This calmed everyone down except me. I needed a better answer, so I did some study. Here is the scripture I am referring to in Ephesians 5:21–22: "submitting to one another in the fear of God. Wives, submit to your own husbands, as to the Lord."

However, in the Greek text the word *submit* does not appear twice. It is a part of that sentence that begins in the preceding verse. It looks like this in English: "Submit yourselves one to another out of reverence to Christ, wives to their own husbands as to the Lord."[70]

So here is my brief conclusion. The biblical foundation for marriage is dependent upon submission that is absolutely and totally voluntary, one to the other, because the two are one. They are one, so one spouse is not under or over the other; they are equal. It is the only structure strong enough to withstand the tests that come to marriages. Honestly, read any marriage manual, ask any marriage counsellor; anything less than submit to one another will not be a successful marriage. Grace and faith, hope, love and wisdom abounds to both husband and wife[71] and true love is without hypocrisy,[72] and it esteems the other better than themselves.[73] "True love suffers long and is kind; love does not envy; love does not parade itself, is not puffed up; does not behave rudely, does not seek its own, is not provoked, and thinks no evil" (1 Corinthians 13:4, 5).

Q: Are women more easily deceived than men?

A: Here is a stupid lie I never really believed but tried very hard to, because I wanted to be the best Christian in the world, and because the Pastor said it—that women are more easily deceived than men because Eve was deceived, implying that a woman could not be trusted to take any leadership position in the church without a husband to check up on her deceptions. Well, how about no! The issue is not about gender; anyone can be deceived, which is why the great apostle Paul says to everyone to grow up,[74] so we can recognize every false doctrine or traditions that men invent according to the basic principles of the world and not according to Christ.[75] When did Jesus ever treat women as if they were easily deceived? The Bible encourages everyone to rightly divide the word of truth. [76]

Q: If I step outside my husband's covering, will the devil get me?

A: Here's another lie I once believed: if I stepped outside my husband's covering, (I was never sure what this actually meant anyway) the devil would get me. This then surely is an insult to a mighty God and everything He has done for us. It is like saying that the Father, the Lord Jesus Christ and Holy Spirit, are not enough for wives and that they need a husband to provide covering/spiritual protection as well. To be honest, I cannot find any scripture that backs this up. Furthermore, what about Psalm 91:4, which was written before the devil was defeated by the death of Jesus? "He shall cover you with His feathers, and under His wings you shall take refuge; His truth shall be your shield and buckler."

Because a husband and a wife are one they come against the forces of darkness together, they submit to God and resist evil and it flees.[77] And what about single women? There is no record of Almighty God having to get permission from Joseph or Mary's father so Mary could give birth to the Savior of the world. Jesus did not secure a male covering for Mary Magdalene, a single woman, before he told her to go and tell the others about His resurrection. Jesus Himself commissioned her and the other women at the tomb also, and that is all anyone needs. We are all sons and daughters, children of God and joint heirs with Jesus, equally redeemed and equally needing redeeming.

Q: What do we do with the lies we have been told?

A: It is truth that sets us free, then it must be lies that imprison us, so that is a good reason to know the truth. Once you have recognized the lie, just don't believe it anymore, because when you believe something about God that is not true, it affects how you see God and how you see yourself.

Afterword

The greatest and most compelling reason for us to discover our determination is because life was never meant to be easy. It presents us with challenges and situations that need determination to get through. It is our determination that pushes us to use our faith to see the impossible, to go the distance, to know God personally, and to know that we have a Father God who is good and who loves us, no matter what. It takes determination to know the truth, because the truth makes you free and determines how you see God and how you see yourself.

"Legacy of Love that Lasts"

Colleen McLean

You need Jesus, who empowers
you to lead with love.
He gives you wisdom that
you can only dream of.
Keeping the law cannot empower you;
Trying harder might just see you through,
But to lead with love like Jesus did,
You need His love, grace, and
righteousness within.
God is so real and able to be experienced.
His love for you is not mysterious.
It is a gift which is freely given.
It is not achieved by ambition.
But simply by faith and changing your mind,
Like the song, you can sing, "I once was blind
But now I see that my Creator's
eyes are always on me."
So for all the leaders who set
their lives to the task,
Jesus is your legacy of love that lasts.

Endnotes

1   Peter 3:15.
2   Romans 8:35–39.

Chapter 1

3   1 John 1:7.

Chapter 2

4   Galatians 3:26–29.
5   Luke 8:24; Acts 27:18.
6   Acts 10:25.
7   Ephesians 1:4; 1 Peter 2:9.
8   John 4.
9   Galatians 3:28.
10   Romans 8:35–39.
11   1 John 1:7.
12   Genesis 1:1; Ephesians 2:20.

13 John 17:3.

14 Galatians 3:28.

Chapter 8

15 Hebrews 5:9; 12:2.

16 Ephesians 4:13.

17 Psalm 139.

18 Genesis 1; Psalm 33:6, 9; Hebrews 11:3.

19 Acts 17:24.

20 Hebrews 1:3.

21 https://en.wikipedia.org/wiki/Biblical_manuscript.

22 Romans 8:28.

23 Matthew 4:45.

24 1 John 4:4, 5:4.

25 Genesis 45:7.

26 Matthew 8:17; 1 Peter 2:24.

27 1 John 1:5.

28 Hebrews 12:6.

29 His death on the cross changed everything.

30 1 Peter 2:24; Matthew 8:17.

31 Matthew 12:14; 15:1–4.

32 John 3:16.

33 Romans 3:20; Acts 7:53.

34 Ephesians 4:26–27.

35 Matthew 5:29.

36 Matthew 25:41.

37 2 Peter 2:4.

38 John 10:3.

39 Psalm 44:21.

40 Psalm 94:11.

41 Matthew 6:8.

42 1 Corinthians 2:10.

43 Acts 2:23, Acts 4:28.

44   2 Timothy 1:7.

45   1 Thessalonians 4:3, 7.

46   Matthew 8:17; Hebrews 4:15.

47   1 John 1:5.

48   Matthew 23

49   "Current neuroscientific and quantum physics research confirms that our thoughts change our brains daily. It is called "self-directed neuroplasticity," which describes the principle that deep thinking changes brain structure and function." (Leaf, Dr. Caroline, *Switch on Your Brain: How to Switch on Your Brain.* Baker Books: Grand Rapids, MI, 2013.)

50   Numbers 23:19; I Samuel 15:29; 2 Timothy 2:13; Hebrews 6:18; James 1:13, 17.

51   Matthew 3:9; 26:53.

52   Deuteronomy 7:2–9.

53   Joshua 6:19.

54   https://en.wikipedia.org/wiki/Atomic_bombings_of_ Hiroshima_and_Nagasaki.

55   2 Samuel 5:6–7.

56   Luke 6:27.

57   https://en.wikipedia.org/wiki/Nebraska_Man.

58   https://www.livescience.com.

59   Exodus 30:13; Deuteronomy 5:17.

60   Matthew 19:5; 1 Corinthians 6:16.

61   Deuteronomy 21:15.

62   Judges 4:4–5.

63   Acts 18:26; Romans 16:3–5.

64   Roman 16:1–2.

65   Romans 16:7.

66   Acts 16:40.

67   Luke 4:18.

68   Luke 8:3.

69   Galatians 3:28.

70   http://biblehub.com/text/ephesians/5–21.htm.

71 Ephesians 1:7; 1 Corinthians 13:13

72 Romans 12:9

73 Philippians 12:3

74 Ephesians 4:14.

75 Colossians 2:8.

76 1 Timothy 2:15.

77 James 4:7.

Printed in the United States
By Bookmasters